Who saw Beauty cry, and failed to hold her left hand?

MEDITATIONS FOR WOMEN

DIANNE CIKUSA

Cataloguing-in-Publication entry is available from the National Library of Australia: http://catalogue.nla.gov.au/

Title: Who saw Beauty cry, and failed to hold her left hand?

Subtitle: Meditations for women

Author: Cikusa, Dianne, 1973–

ISBNs: 978-0-6484923-4-4 (paperback)

Subjects: BODY, MIND & SPIRIT: Inspiration & Personal
          Growth; SELF-HELP: Personal Growth / Self-Esteem;
          Meditations; PHILOSOPHY: Metaphysics

Cover and internal images under license from Adobe Stock

Cover design by Ally Mosher @ allymosher.com

Published by Mignon Press, 2020

PO Box 922, Katoomba NSW 2780

mignon
PRESS

Also by Dianne Cikusa:

The Rain Sermon: Le Sermon de la Pluie

The Sea In-Between

Hope and Substance

Be ever so humble
and ever so grateful,

yet allow no
discordant person
to diminish you

and no
uncordial situation
to corrupt you.

Who saw Beauty cry, and failed to hold her left hand?

You are only upset because you tolerate that which you can choose to walk away from.

Who saw Beauty cry, and failed to hold her left hand?

4

Our own spirit is conceivably the best companion we will ever have at our benevolent disposal.

6   Who saw Beauty cry, and failed to hold her left hand?

To obtain valuable
answers, first prompt
some worthwhile
questions.

Who saw Beauty cry, and failed to hold her left hand?

No one can take your
living journey away
from you; not the
pain, not the wisdom.

Who saw Beauty cry, and failed to hold her left hand?

There is no good day
and no bad day --
just a day in life.

Who saw Beauty cry, and failed to hold her left hand?

'Inner power' is perhaps the truest measure of one's quality of life.

Who saw Beauty cry, and failed to hold her left hand?

Genuinely empowered people do not need to tell anyone what to do.

Who saw Beauty cry, and failed to hold her left hand?

To release control, you
may need to stand
down from God's
pedestal.

Who saw Beauty cry, and failed to hold her left hand?

Look into the abyss...
of what you have been
ignorantly flushing
out to sea.

Who saw Beauty cry, and failed to hold her left hand?

Acknowledge those
natural elements
residing beneficially in
your body.

Who saw Beauty cry, and failed to hold her left hand?

Your life is
unconsciously perfect.
Now make it
consciously so.

Who saw Beauty cry, and failed to hold her left hand?

How can there be boredom, when there is always more to discover about oneself?

Who saw Beauty cry, and failed to hold her left hand?

Whenever your mind is involved in what it believes to be a complex problem, simplify it so it can be explained in terms of your fear and your death.

Who saw Beauty cry, and failed to hold her left hand?

From chaos emerges
newest possibilities.

Who saw Beauty cry, and failed to hold her left hand?

When perfect circles
made love with
relevant squares, we
found a synonymous
balance.

Who saw Beauty cry, and failed to hold her left hand?

Whether you accomplish it all or not, isn't it enough just to be alive?

Who saw Beauty cry, and failed to hold her left hand?

Inner stillness is a
moon that keeps
changing, yet stays
eternally mesmerising.

Who saw Beauty cry, and failed to hold her left hand?

An honourable
friendship respects
the variability of
opinions.

Who saw Beauty cry, and failed to hold her left hand?

Love the human being
who holds your shame,
and fails to laugh.

40

Who saw Beauty cry, and failed to hold her left hand?

If nothing could offend you, heaven would be yours.

Who saw Beauty cry, and failed to hold her left hand?

Think twice before
speaking; once for
Self, once for Soul.

Who saw Beauty cry, and failed to hold her left hand?

Don't cry over spilled milk, just wipe it up with more water.

Who saw Beauty cry, and failed to hold her left hand?

If you'd been
listening to the pain,
you might have
learned for the cure.

48

Who saw Beauty cry, and failed to hold her left hand?

Expectation is at the root of all of our disconcerted betrayal.

Who saw Beauty cry, and failed to hold her left hand?

Don't blame the symptom for the cause of an unresolved feeling.

Who saw Beauty cry, and failed to hold her left hand?

Where you've borrowed

a sympathetic ear,

respect its volume.

Who saw Beauty cry, and failed to hold her left hand?

'Displeasure' is purely an attitude to the misfortunes of Life.

Who saw Beauty cry, and failed to hold her left hand?

Resentment -- is wishing wealth away from the rest of the world.

Who saw Beauty cry, and failed to hold her left hand?

Fighting for justice...
is sometimes fighting
to self-justify.

Who saw Beauty cry, and failed to hold her left hand?

Learn where <u>not</u> to dig; alliances and camaraderie can be lost that way.

Who saw Beauty cry, and failed to hold her left hand?

Don't take life so
seriously!
(Only don't forget to
grow in the spiritual
sense either).

Who saw Beauty cry, and failed to hold her left hand?

Nothing is so
impossible, with a
little organised time
in our favour.

Who saw Beauty cry, and failed to hold her left hand?

We couldn't see the 'whole' problem until we emptied of its pieces.

Who saw Beauty cry, and failed to hold her left hand?

Wonder stayed
attentively behind you,
even when you blindly
kept going.

Who saw Beauty cry, and failed to hold her left hand?

God in one thought:

Thank you!

72

Who saw Beauty cry, and failed to hold her left hand?

Stress is volubly
telling your life, not
quietly being your
person.

Who saw Beauty cry, and failed to hold her left hand?

Consciously shrink
what 'needs' and
abundance will expand.

Who saw Beauty cry, and failed to hold her left hand?

Where our inner faith
is lacking, we may
argue the world.

Who saw Beauty cry, and failed to hold her left hand?

Spirit knowledge
guides you.
Spirit wisdom
releases you.

Who saw Beauty cry, and failed to hold her left hand?

Backtrack your own befuddled path, since nobody else walked it for you.

Who saw Beauty cry, and failed to hold her left hand?

Saying 'no' sustains
one's power of
rejection.

Who saw Beauty cry, and failed to hold her left hand?

'Free time' was how

you already used it.

Who saw Beauty cry, and failed to hold her left hand?

Observe *why* the emotional blocks are there, and you'll see the purpose in waiting for them to clear.

Who saw Beauty cry, and failed to hold her left hand?

Paranoia is also an
intense psychic trip.

Who saw Beauty cry, and failed to hold her left hand?

Where it didn't feel good, you began to judge your preference.

Who saw Beauty cry, and failed to hold her left hand?

Ugliness -- is just a
bad mood.

Who saw Beauty cry, and failed to hold her left hand?

A bit of fear won't
kill *all* of you.

Who saw Beauty cry, and failed to hold her left hand?

Mutual respect
attains when we are
not afraid to be seen
'as' each other.

Who saw Beauty cry, and failed to hold her left hand?

Listen to the
advocating world,
then peaceably ignore
what it tells you.

Who saw Beauty cry, and failed to hold her left hand?

Provoke self-worth --
wherever an outside
approval is not
forthcoming.

Who saw Beauty cry, and failed to hold her left hand?

Recycle one addiction
before you go and
feed another.

Who saw Beauty cry, and failed to hold her left hand?

Although enlightenment was told to you a thousand times, you were choosing out the voices.

Who saw Beauty cry, and failed to hold her left hand?

Routine repeats, until
we are no longer
despising it.

Who saw Beauty cry, and failed to hold her left hand?

The masculine

refreshes our personal

power;

the feminine nurtures

our global soul.

Who saw Beauty cry, and failed to hold her left hand?

The astral body...
is in every place you
left it behind.

Who saw Beauty cry, and failed to hold her left hand?

Inner reflection:

Why is my outward
body looking like the
denial of my mind?

Who saw Beauty cry, and failed to hold her left hand?

Eventually, you'll get around to using that procrastinating spare tyre.

Who saw Beauty cry, and failed to hold her left hand?

We learn how to
moderate through
excess, and how to
find value through
depletion.

Who saw Beauty cry, and failed to hold her left hand?

What you 'don't' like
in the world does not
cease to exist.

Who saw Beauty cry, and failed to hold her left hand?

Self-understanding is also the basis for our intuitive compassion.

Who saw Beauty cry, and failed to hold her left hand?

'Higher purpose' is meaningfully putting all your spirit-eggs in one basket.

Who saw Beauty cry, and failed to hold her left hand?

Poor 'body image' is in part an emotional issue.

Who saw Beauty cry, and failed to hold her left hand?

Freedom is in that
instance when you are
so angry, you could
laugh.

Who saw Beauty cry, and failed to hold her left hand?

Hatred cannot touch joy, but love can be gently touching to hate.

Who saw Beauty cry, and failed to hold her left hand?

Child's birthday --
is also celebrating
mother's annual
birthing day.

Who saw Beauty cry, and failed to hold her left hand?

If the energy isn't
you, then why do you
react to it?

Who saw Beauty cry, and failed to hold her left hand?

Any external sermon towards self-improvement should read first and foremost to oneself.

Who saw Beauty cry, and failed to hold her left hand?

Watch where your
happiness pushes too
strongly in the face
of another.

Who saw Beauty cry, and failed to hold her left hand?

Think to do it wrong,
then feel to do it
right.

Who saw Beauty cry, and failed to hold her left hand?

While one event is keeping you busy, the restful thing is slipping away.

Who saw Beauty cry, and failed to hold her left hand?

If you'd gotten everything you'd wanted, you would have missed the small point.

Who saw Beauty cry, and failed to hold her left hand?

Romance is one thing;
Love can be quite the
opposite.

Who saw Beauty cry, and failed to hold her left hand?

Where blame went
astray, so too did the
heart.

Who saw Beauty cry, and failed to hold her left hand?

Cry hard, until you become a single teardrop.

Who saw Beauty cry, and failed to hold her left hand?

No matter how much
you tried covering it
up, the insecurity was
resolutely breaking
through.

Who saw Beauty cry, and failed to hold her left hand?

Creative motivation --

is a continual process

of reaching sublime

inner heights.

Who saw Beauty cry, and failed to hold her left hand?

Use better your
'past mind' for
establishing an
unshakeable present
experience.

Who saw Beauty cry, and failed to hold her left hand?

Enjoy a positive effect (irrespective of whether or not it will last).

Who saw Beauty cry, and failed to hold her left hand?

Before you next fill up, consider the comings and goings of all you are appreciably doing.

Who saw Beauty cry, and failed to hold her left hand?

Someone else took
notes whenever you
were talking to make
yourself look smart,
or sound pretty.

Who saw Beauty cry, and failed to hold her left hand?

Envy -- is hating
something it
desperately wants.

Who saw Beauty cry, and failed to hold her left hand?

Whilst complexity struggles to keep up with life, spirituality keeps abreast.

Who saw Beauty cry, and failed to hold her left hand?

Be mindful insofar as what you 'say' and what you 'do' are signifying two opposing sagas.

Who saw Beauty cry, and failed to hold her left hand?

Revere yourself as
female-human.
Respect yourself as
woman-body.

Who saw Beauty cry, and failed to hold her left hand?

Play your
small-sized role in
your tiny-kempt
world.

Who saw Beauty cry, and failed to hold her left hand?

Spirit ecstasy -- is loving everything in a single breath.

Who saw Beauty cry, and failed to hold her left hand?

Transcend possibility...

become it!

Who saw Beauty cry, and failed to hold her left hand?

Nothing really
matters, except that
we are wanting it to.

Who saw Beauty cry, and failed to hold her left hand?

Maintain your energy
in miniature spheres,
so you can radiate
outwards from an
enduring inner core.

Who saw Beauty cry, and failed to hold her left hand?

Mind will engage the
soul's accompanying
awareness.

Who saw Beauty cry, and failed to hold her left hand?

Simple enlightenment
is when the body
grows quiet.

Who saw Beauty cry, and failed to hold her left hand?

'Change' is the way in which we continue learning a comparable lesson.

Who saw Beauty cry, and failed to hold her left hand?

So maybe you didn't win, but you are still a beautiful moment.

For information and links, please visit:

www.mignonpress.com